Little Math St[...]

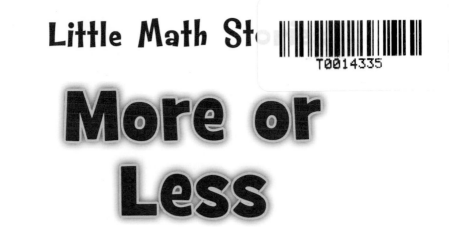

More or Less

By Amanda Gebhardt

 Mom and I get a box of yarn.

There is not a lot of
yarn in the box.

"Help get a box with more,"
Mom said.

Is this more or less?

 It is less. We can get more.

Is this more or less?

 It is less. We can get more.

Is this more or less?

 10

Yes! This is more!

"Mom! Mom! This is more!"

"Yes!" said Mom.
"It is much more!"

We got more yarn.

Word List

math words
more

less

sight words
a   the

I   We

of

r-controlled

/ar/ar	/air/ere	/or/or, ore
yarn	There	more
		or

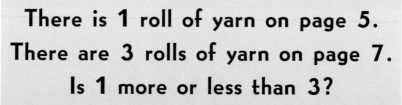

Try It!
There is **1** roll of yarn on page **5**.
There are **3** rolls of yarn on page **7**.
Is **1** more or less than **3**?

14

Mom and I get a box of yarn.

There is not a lot of yarn in the box.

"Help get a box with more," Mom said.

Is this more or less?

It is less. We can get more.

Is this more or less?

It is less. We can get more.

Is this more or less?

Yes! This is more!

"Mom! Mom! This is more!"

"Yes!" said Mom. "It is much more!"

We got more yarn.

CHERRY BLOSSOM PRESS

Published in the United States of America by Cherry Lake Publishing Group
Ann Arbor, Michlgan
www.cherrylakepublishing.com

Photo Credits: Cover: © darksoul72/Shutterstock.com; pages 2, 4, 6, 8, 10–13: © fizkes/
Shutterstock.com; pages 3, 5, 7: © Cherry Lake Publishing; page 9: © donatas1205/
Shutterstock.com; page 15, Back Cover: © Nataliia K/Shutterstock.com

Cherry Blossom Press is an imprint of Cherry Lake Publishing Group.

Library of Congress Cataloging-in-Publication Data has been filed and is available at catalog.loc.gov.

Cherry Lake Publishing Group would like to acknowledge the work of the Partnership for 21st Century
Learning, a Network of Battelle for Kids. Please visit http://www.battelleforkids.org/networks/p21
for more information.

Printed in the United States of America
Corporate Graphics

Amanda Gebhardt is a curriculum writer and editor and a life-long learner. She lives in Ann Arbor,
Michigan, with her husband, two kids, and one playful pup named Cookie.